The Wren-Boys

Carol Ann Duffy

Illustrated by Dermot Flynn

PICADOR

First published 2015 by Picador
an imprint of Pan Macmillan
20 New Wharf Road, London N1 9RR
Associated companies throughout the world
www.panmacmillan.com

ISBN 978-1-4472-7148-2

1 3 5 7 9 8 6 4 2

A CIP catalogue record for this book is available from the British Library.

Manufactured in Spain by Graficas Estella

For Theo Dorgan and Paula Meehan —
Sláinte.

The Wren-Boys

The old year, a tear in the eye of time;
frost on the blackthorn, the ditches glamorous
with rime; on the inbreath of air,
the long, thoughtful pause before snow.

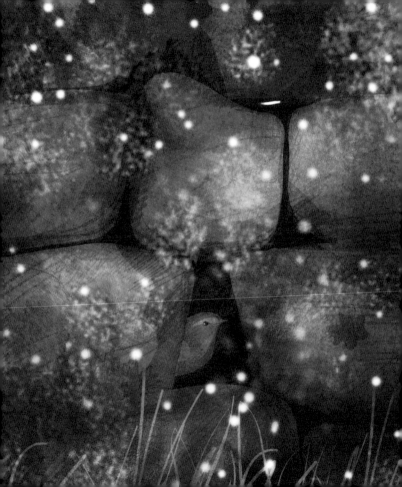

A star on the brow of a mule in a field
and the mule nuzzling the drystone wall
where a wren, size of a child's lost purse,
hides in a hole. St. Stephen's Day.

Eight bells from the Church. Next to the Church,
the Inn. Next to the Inn, and opposite,
a straight furlong of dwellings. End of the line,
a farm. Top of the hill, the Big House –

everywhere musky with peat from the first fires
as though the hour had started the day
with a neat malt; like your man has here
who bangs on door after door with his holly-stick.

Quick boys! Up for the wren! Then the Wren-Boys
flinging open the doors in their green-laced boots,
daft caps, red neckerchiefs, with cudgels and nets;
one with a cage held aloft on the tip of a ribboned staff.

Hedge-bandit, song-bomb, dart-beak, the wren
hops in the thicket, flirt-eye; shy, brave,
grubbing, winter's scamp, but more than itself –
ten requisite grams of the world's weight.

And here's the craic: that the little bird
had betrayed a saint with its song,
or stolen a ride on an eagle's back
to fly highest; traitor and cheat.

But poets named it *Dryw*, druid and wren,
sought its hermit tune for a muse;
sweethearts thought it a foolproof blessing for love.
Which was true for the wren? None of the above.

Over the wall, over the field, was the wood
to where the Wren-Boys stomped in a singing gang:
We'll chase him from bush to bush
and from tree to tree. One had a fiddle,

one had a penny-whistle, another a drum,
one had thirty feathers poked in his hat.
So through the holly, the hazel, the ash,
the brackeny floor, they hunted the wren.

Five hours in, they had startled a fox
which ran like the hounds; had bagged a nest
with five blue unhatched eggs; scarpered
from a cache of poteen stashed in an oak.

On a twig, a robin watched them go,
safe in its myth. It had started to snow
and the boots of the boys blotted the page of the field
as they made for the margins – the ditches and hedgerows.

The priest was supping a pint of stout in the pub,
a small icon of his holy self, clocking the top shelf.
The farmer was sat by the fire with his dog.
Four widows were sharing a Christmas nog.

And the sky went falling, falling, down to the earth
till a lad was sent to fetch the mule to its stall,
and the bell had a muffled, sorrowful sound
and up at the Big House all the lights came on.

And the clouds came grieving, grieving, down to the land,
but could they find *that feckin wran*,
as they thrashed, poked, joshed and joked
along the lane where weddings and funerals came.

Who it was who plonked his arse on a stile
and yanked the wipe from his neck, the plumes
from his brother's hat, to fashion a dummy bird,
no living man can tell; nor hear their boisterous glee

as they caged the raggedy wren and swaggered,
whistling, fiddling, drumming, back up the road –
The wren, the wren, the Lord of all birds,
On St. Stephen's Day was caught on the furze . . .

Sing holly, sing ivy, sing ivy, sing holly,
a drop just to drink it will drown melancholy . . .
away round the bend in dwindling violet light
into their given lives, snow-ghosts, gone . . .

to boast at each house with a verse, a sock
for farthings, threepennies, sixpences, florins;
then toast that the wren was out with the old
and in with the new was the robin.

Which would have been news to the wren,
had it understood claptrap, mythology, fable,
warm in its communal roost in the stable
over the heads of the dozing beasts –

while the Wren-Boys boozed and danced at the Inn;
one with a widow, one with the farmer's daughter,
one with a sweetheart, one with a sozzled priest.
Later, the snow settled, a star in the east.

Also by Carol Ann Duffy and available from Picador